The Exercise of Our Spirit

WITNESS LEE

Living Stream Ministry
Anaheim, CA • www.lsm.org

First Edition, January 2005.

ISBN 0-7363-2816-5

Published by

Living Stream Ministry
2431 W. La Palma Ave., Anaheim, CA 92801 U.S.A.
P. O. Box 2121, Anaheim, CA 92814 U.S.A.

Printed in the United States of America

05 06 07 08 09 10 11 / 9 8 7 6 5 4 3 2 1

CONTENTS

PREFACE

This book is composed of messages given by Brother Witness Lee during the summer training of 1966 in Los Angeles, California. These messages were not reviewed by the speaker.

Chapter One

DEALING WITH OUR INWARD PARTS FOR THE EXERCISE OF OUR SPIRIT

(1)

Scripture Reading: 1 Tim. 4:7-8; 3:16; 1:4; 2 Tim. 4:22; 1:7; 1 Tim. 1:5, 19; 3:9; 2 Tim. 1:3

The two main items dealt with in the writings of the apostle Paul are Christ as the life of the church and the church as the expression of Christ. The writings of Paul are in two sections. The first is from Romans through 2 Thessalonians. This section deals with the vision concerning the life and nature of the church, revealing what the church is, the content of the church, Christ as the life of the church, and the church as the expression of Christ. After this clear definition and revelation, the second section—from 1 Timothy through Philemon—deals with the practice of the Christian life and church life. The best way to present a message concerning a certain matter is first to give a definition, vision, and revelation of that matter and then to present the way to practice it. In the same way, Paul's principle in his writings is first to give a definition of the Christian life and church life and then to tell us the way to practice this.

The way to practice the Christian life and church life is to exercise ourselves unto godliness. First Timothy 4:7 and 8 say, "The profane and old-womanish myths refuse, and exercise yourself unto godliness. For bodily exercise is profitable for a little, but godliness is profitable for all things, having promise of the present life and of that which is to come." The Greek word for *exercise* here is the root of the word *gymnastics.* Paul wrote this Epistle during the era of the Greek

Olympics, which included gymnastics, bodily exercise which is good for physical health. Here the apostle Paul used this word to say that we need another kind of "gymnastics," one that is related not to the physical body but to godliness. Bodily exercise is profitable only for a little, but the second kind of exercise is profitable both for today and forever, for the present life and for that which is to come. Therefore, we need to pay more attention to this kind of exercise.

What is the second kind of exercise in 1 Timothy 4? It is not the exercise of our mentality, for we have already received this from our schooling. From our youth we received learning for the exercise of our mind, through elementary, junior high, senior high, college, and even graduate school. Besides bodily and mental exercise, what other kind of exercise do we need? It must be that the second kind of exercise mentioned by the apostle Paul is the exercise of our human spirit.

GODLINESS BEING THE MANIFESTATION OF GOD IN THE FLESH

In order to know what the exercise unto godliness is, we must first see what godliness is in the two Epistles to Timothy. The definition of godliness is in 1 Timothy 3:16, which says, "Confessedly, great is the mystery of godliness: He who was manifested in the flesh, / Justified in the Spirit, / Seen by angels, / Preached among the nations, / Believed on in the world, / Taken up in glory." After the word *godliness* there is a colon, indicating that what follows is the definition. Godliness is God-likeness, that is, God manifested in the flesh. According to the context, this verse refers not only to Christ Himself but also to the church. The previous verse says, "If I delay, I write that you may know how one ought to conduct himself in the house of God, which is the church of the living God, the pillar and base of the truth" (v. 15). In principle, the church is both the house of the living God, the pillar and base of the truth, and the mystery of godliness—the manifestation of God in the flesh. While Christ was on the earth, He was God manifested in the flesh. Likewise, the church today is in the flesh, but God is manifested in it.

We need to keep in mind that godliness implies that God

is manifested in us, the flesh. Godliness is more than simply having the likeness of God. After Adam was created, he had the likeness of God because he was made in the image of God (Gen. 1:26). However, without partaking of the tree of life, Adam was not able to manifest God. He could not express God in reality because he did not have God living within him. For God to be manifested in the flesh in a living way, for Him to express Himself through us, requires that He live in us. Often the newspapers print a picture of the President. We may say that the President is expressed in the newspapers, but he is not expressed in a living way, since there is no life in a photograph. Similarly, we do not express God in the way of a photograph. We are the manifestation of God and express Him in a living way because He lives in us. This expression and manifestation of God is godliness.

THE MYSTERY OF GODLINESS BEING GOD'S ECONOMY TO BUILD HIMSELF INTO US

First Timothy 1:4 says, "Nor to give heed to myths and unending genealogies, which produce questionings rather than God's economy, which is in faith." God's economy is His building economy, the economy for His building. Today God is building Himself into us. God's intention as revealed in the entire Bible is to work Himself into man. In type, the forty-eight boards of the tabernacle were built into the overlaying gold (Exo. 26:15-23, 29). It is in the overlaying gold that the boards became part of God's building. The boards were built up with the gold, and the gold was built up with the boards. Gold typifies the divine nature of God. Today we are being built up as one in God's divine nature (2 Pet. 1:4). Similarly, the precious stones on the shoulder plates and breastplate of the high priest were enclosed in settings of gold (Exo. 28:9-12, 15-20). The stones were built into the gold, and the gold was built with them; they and the gold were built up together as one. This is the way that God's building is constituted.

God's work of building is to build Himself into us and with us so that we may be built together as one in Him. This is God's building economy. The word *economy* in Greek is also the word for dispensation, or governmental arrangement. This dispensation and arrangement is for God's building. God is dispensing Himself into His many children so that He may build Himself into us and with us so that He and we would be one. God's building economy is the mystery of godliness. In the whole universe, this economy is a mystery, not only to the unbelievers but also to many Christians (Eph. 3:9). Many Christians say that God saved us simply because He loved us and wanted to deliver us from hell and bring us to heaven. Not many are clear concerning the mystery of godliness, that God's intention is to dispense Himself into us and build Himself together with us as one. This is a true mystery, a mystery not only to the angels but also to man. However, through the revelation in the word of God, this mystery has been made known to us (Eph. 3:4-5). It is no longer only a mystery; it is a reality.

THE EXERCISE UNTO GODLINESS BEING THE EXERCISE OF OUR HUMAN SPIRIT

By all of the preceding points, we can be clear that godliness is God manifested in the flesh. Therefore, to exercise ourselves unto godliness is to exercise so that God may be manifested in us. Bodily exercise does not help us to have God manifested in us. Likewise, mere mental exercise does not avail for God to express Himself within us. Therefore, the exercise mentioned in 1 Timothy 4:7 must be the exercise of our human spirit. It is by the exercise of our spirit that God is manifested in us.

Second Timothy 4:22 says, "The Lord be with your spirit. Grace be with you." This verse is the closing word of the two Epistles to Timothy. Since a person's closing word stresses the main point of his writing, Paul's central point in these Epistles must be related to our spirit. This verse tells us that God today is in our spirit. Moreover, it indicates that the One within us is not only God Himself but also Christ, the Lord. To mention the Lord implies very much. God did not come into man directly. First, He was incarnated to be the man Jesus (John 1:14). This man went to the cross and was crucified to accomplish our redemption, and then He was buried.

Following this He was resurrected, and in His resurrection He was glorified (Luke 24:26, 46). In incarnation God became Jesus, and through death and in resurrection and ascension He as Jesus was made Christ, the Lord (Acts 2:36). Moreover, this Christ became a life-giving Spirit (1 Cor. 15:45b). This Spirit who is Christ Himself came into our human spirit. Now Christ is in our spirit, as 2 Timothy 4:22 says, "The Lord be with your spirit."

God did not come into us directly without incarnation, redemption, resurrection, or ascension. Rather, God came into us as Christ, who is God plus man, with the human life and nature, crucifixion for redemption, resurrection, and ascension. Now He is the life-giving Spirit, and as such a One He comes into us, that is, into our spirit. Therefore, in order to exercise unto godliness, to be the manifestation of God in the flesh, we must exercise our spirit.

HAVING A SPIRIT OF POWER, OF LOVE, AND OF SOBERMINDEDNESS

Second Timothy 1:7 says, "God has not given us a spirit of cowardice, but of power and of love and of sobermindedness." The spirit mentioned here is not the Holy Spirit; it is our human spirit. God has given us a spirit of three items: power, love, and sobermindedness. Why does this verse speak of three items, not two or four? It is because the soul that surrounds our spirit is of three parts—the mind, the emotion, and the will (Prov. 2:10; Psa. 139:14; Lam. 3:20; S. S. 1:7a; 2 Sam. 5:8; Psa. 86:4; Job 6:7; 7:15; 1 Chron. 22:19a). These three parts must be related to our spirit in a proper way. The spirit of power is related to the will. Our will must be subdued by the spirit and submissive to the spirit. A spirit of power is a spirit of a subdued, submissive will. If our will is independent from the spirit, it may be stubborn and hard, but it is not strong in a proper way. Sometimes we may say that a certain person has a strong will. In actuality, we may be using the wrong word. That person's will may be hard and stubborn, but it is not strong in a proper way unless it is subdued by and submissive to his spirit. Such a will becomes powerful under the control of the spirit. A martyr is strong in his will because at the time of his martyrdom his will is completely submissive to his spirit. When our will is subdued by and submissive to our spirit, it becomes strong, and our spirit becomes a spirit of power.

The reason that our spirit is often weak when we come to the meetings is that our will is too independent of the Lord; it has not been subdued by the Lord and made submissive to Him. An independent will causes our spirit to be weakened. The more submissive and obedient our will is, the stronger and more powerful we will be in our spirit. Whenever we are rebellious to the Lord, our spirit is weakened and even deadened, but when we are submissive and obedient to the Lord, our spirit rises up and becomes powerful. A spirit of power is a spirit of a will that is subdued and submissive.

We also need a spirit of love. We may have a will that is subdued and submissive to our spirit yet still be cold in our emotions. It may be easy for us to be cold toward others, condemning them and considering that they are rebellious. This means that we are unbalanced and out of proportion. We should have a spirit not only of power but also of love. Consider the Lord Jesus. While He was on this earth, His will was submissive and He was obedient to the Father, so His spirit was strong. However, His spirit was also full of love. He had a strong spirit, not only of power but also of love. Toward Satan, the evil one, His spirit was strong, but toward the sinful ones His spirit was full of love and sympathy. This is the proper balance. We need love to balance power. Love is a matter of our emotion, so we need to be not only submissive but also "emotional." If we do not know how to laugh or weep, we cannot be spiritual. It is wrong for a brother never to laugh but always to have a cold face, an expression without warmth. We need a spirit of love to balance our spirit of power.

To be a balanced person is not easy. We may realize our need to be balanced but become too emotional; we will then need to be balanced again. We should not love people foolishly. Love can blind us and cause us to be foolish. Therefore, we also must have a spirit of sobermindedness. We must love others, not foolishly but properly, with a clear and sober mind. Hosea 7:8 tells us that Ephraim was a cake "not turned."

It is wrong to bake a cake on one side only without turning it over. The best way to bake something is to turn it several times. We need to "turn" our spirit continually to be balanced. Our will must be submissive, our emotion must be exercised to love others, and our mind must be sober, clear, and proper. Sometimes brothers and sisters spoil people by their foolish and natural love. This is because they have love but are short of sobermindedness. They love with a foolish mind, not with a sober mind. We must love others soberly so that they will receive a benefit from our love; otherwise, they may be damaged and even deadened by our love.

To exercise our spirit so that God may be manifested in us requires that we have a spirit with a submissive will, a loving emotion, and a fine, sober, clear, and proper mind. In order to exercise our spirit, we need to adjust all these inward parts. To exercise our spirit that God may be manifested in us is not simply to pray. We must also be adjusted in our will, emotion, and mind. If our will, emotion, or mind is wrong, we cannot have a good exercise of a proper spirit.

God requires that we exercise unto godliness, which is simply God manifested in us. As we have seen, God is Christ, who is in our spirit. Therefore, we must exercise our spirit. This spirit must be a spirit of power, of love, and of sobermindedness. Our spirit is surrounded by our will, emotion, and mind; if these three parts are not adjusted and proper, we cannot have a proper spirit. We should not think that to exercise the spirit is merely to go to the Lord or to the meetings to pray. Of course, we need to pray, but we must also be adjusted in our inward parts, the parts of our soul—the will, the emotion, and the mind. We must check as to whether our will is submissive or stubborn, soft or hard. Likewise, if our emotions are too cold, they must be adjusted, and our mind must be enlightened, sober, and clear.

HAVING A CONSCIENCE THAT IS BOTH GOOD AND PURE

First Timothy 1:5 says, "The end of the charge is love out of a pure heart and out of a good conscience and out of unfeigned faith." In order to exercise our spirit, we must have love, a pure heart, a good conscience, and unfeigned faith. If we lack any of these, we will not be able to exercise our spirit in a proper way. Once again, this means that to exercise our spirit we must deal with every part of our inner being. Verse 19 says, "Holding faith and a good conscience, concerning which some, thrusting these away, have become shipwrecked regarding the faith." Not holding a good conscience causes us to be like a wrecked ship. The conscience is the leading part of the spirit (Rom. 8:16; cf. 9:1). If our conscience is wrong, we cannot have a proper spirit; our spirit will be not exercised but deadened.

First Timothy 3:9 says, "Holding the mystery of the faith in a pure conscience," and 2 Timothy 1:3 begins, "I thank God, whom I serve from my forefathers in a pure conscience." For the exercise of our spirit, we need not only a good conscience but also a pure conscience. We may illustrate the difference between a good conscience and a pure conscience in the following way. If we do something wrong before God or man, we will have an evil conscience, a conscience with offense and condemnation. After we deal with the wrongdoing by applying the cleansing of the Lord's blood, we will have a conscience that is cleansed, without offense, and without condemnation. This is a good conscience. However, we may still not be purely for God and for His will. What we seek may be good and not sinful, but it may be something other than God Himself. This mixture indicates that we do not have a pure heart to seek only God Himself. If our heart is not pure and single, our conscience also will not be pure. The seeking of our heart changes the condition of our conscience. If our conscience is only good but not pure, we will not be able to serve God in an adequate way. In order to serve God, we need a conscience that is both good and pure, a conscience from a heart that seeks after God alone.

A brother may be not only for God but also for the work of the gospel. His heart is divided between two things. Because he cares more for the gospel work than for the Lord, the gospel is a substitute for the Lord in this brother's life and work. It is something for the Lord, but it is not the Lord Himself. If this brother does something sinful, he will have an evil conscience, but because he believes that the gospel work is good, his conscience does not condemn him. Therefore, he has a good conscience, but he does not have a pure conscience. When we deal with our heart to make it pure and single, our heart causes our conscience to also be simple, single, and pure. Then we have a pure conscience before God. This kind of pure conscience will condemn us if we care more for a work than for the Lord.

ALL THE ABOVE MATTERS BEING THE PREPARATION FOR THE EXERCISE OF OUR SPIRIT

The exercise of our spirit is for godliness, which is the manifestation of God in the flesh. God is Christ, who is in our spirit, so we need to deal with our spirit. Our spirit must be a spirit of a subdued and submissive will, of a properly exercised emotion, and of a clear, sound, and sober mind. This exercise also requires a good, pure, and single heart, one that seeks only the Lord Himself, and it requires love and faith. All these matters are the preparation for our exercise of the spirit. It is only in the last few years that the Lord has revealed these things to us from the two Epistles of Timothy. We need to fellowship and pray concerning these matters, study all the foregoing verses, and be thoroughly impressed with them. This will thoroughly prepare us to exercise our spirit.

Chapter Two

DEALING WITH OUR INWARD PARTS FOR THE EXERCISE OF OUR SPIRIT

(2)

Scripture Reading: 1 Tim. 4:7-8; 3:16; 2 Tim. 4:22; 1:7; 1 Tim. 1:3-5; 3:9; 2 Tim. 1:3

First Timothy 4:7 and 8 say, "The profane and old-womanish myths refuse, and exercise yourself unto godliness. For bodily exercise is profitable for a little, but godliness is profitable for all things, having promise of the present life and of that which is to come." These verses speak of two kinds of exercise—bodily exercise and the exercise unto godliness. This second exercise refers neither to the body nor to the soul. Rather, it is the exercise of our human spirit. As we saw in the previous chapter, godliness is the manifestation of God in the flesh (3:16). It is God manifested from within us. Second Timothy 4:22 tells us in what part of our being God dwells. This verse says, "The Lord be with your spirit." *The Lord* refers to God plus many items, including incarnation, crucifixion for redemption, resurrection, and ascension. This Lord, who is God with all these items, has come into our spirit. The foregoing verses show that the exercise unto godliness is the exercise of our human spirit. By the exercise of our spirit we touch the Lord so that He may have the way to manifest Himself in us.

THE INWARD PARTS OF OUR BEING RELATED TO THE EXERCISE OF OUR SPIRIT

The first chapters of both 1 and 2 Timothy speak of the inward parts of our being in relation to the exercise of our spirit. Second Timothy 1:7 says, "For God has not given us a spirit of cowardice, but of power and of love and of sobermindedness." This verse implies the three parts of our soul—our will, emotion, and mind. A spirit of power is a spirit with a proper will, a spirit of love is a spirit with a proper emotion, and a spirit of sobermindedness is a spirit with a clear, sober, and sound mind. God has given us not a weak spirit but a powerful, loving, and sober spirit. In saying this, Paul's intention was not merely to tell us something concerning the spirit; it was that we would use our spirit.

Our spirit is encompassed, surrounded, by the three parts of our soul. Therefore, in order to exercise the spirit we must have a subdued and submissive will, a proper emotion, and a clear and sober mind. If all these parts of the soul are under the control of the spirit, the spirit will be powerful, loving, and sober, and it will be released. Otherwise, our soul will hinder the spirit from being released. When the parts of our soul are under the control of the spirit, they become a free course for the spirit to come out and be released.

THE PROBLEM BEING NOT WITH OUR SPIRIT BUT WITH OUR SOUL

Dealing with our inward parts for the exercise of the spirit may be compared to purifying a flow of water. A spring of water may be pure and clean, but if it flows through sulfurous and salty passages, it will be mixed with sulfur and salt. In order to purify the flow of water, the passages must be cleared up. Strictly speaking, the problems related to the exercise of our spirit are problems with either our will, our emotion, or our mind. There is nothing wrong with our spirit. According to the entire New Testament, God has reserved our spirit for Himself and has not allowed His enemy to come into it. ("Defilement of spirit" in 2 Corinthians 7:1 refers not to our human spirit but to defilement by things in the spiritual world, such as idols.) God allowed the devil, Satan, to damage the body and the soul, causing the spirit to be deadened under the influence of the sinful body and fallen soul. However, the Scriptures do not tell us that Satan takes over the human spirit directly. God has drawn a boundary to preserve our human spirit. Therefore, to deal with the spirit is firstly a matter of dealing with the inward parts that surround the spirit.

The passage to our human spirit is our soul with its several parts. If our mind, will, or emotion is wrong, our spirit cannot be in a proper condition. Therefore, we need to deal with all the parts of our soul. Our will must be subdued, our emotion balanced, and our mind made clear. If our will is submissive, our emotion balanced, and our mind clear and sober, our spirit will be powerful, loving, sober, and easily released.

HAVING A PURE HEART AND A GOOD CONSCIENCE

The two Epistles to Timothy speak mainly of one thing: our need to exercise ourselves unto godliness, which is to exercise our human spirit for the manifestation of God in us. The central thought of these two books is that whether we are elders, deacons, or anyone else in the service of the church, we need to exercise our spirit so that God in Christ as the Spirit may be manifested in us.

First Timothy 1:3 through 5 speak of a pure heart and a good conscience. These verses say, "Even as I exhorted you, when I was going into Macedonia, to remain in Ephesus in order that you might charge certain ones not to teach different things nor to give heed to myths and unending genealogies, which produce questionings rather than God's economy, which is in faith. But the end of the charge is love out of a pure heart and out of a good conscience and out of unfeigned faith." The different teachings, myths, and genealogies produce questionings in the mind. That is, they cause people to exercise their mind to question rather than care for God's economy. Therefore, for the exercise unto godliness according to God's economy, which is the mystery of godliness, God manifested in the flesh, we must have a pure heart and a good conscience.

Our Need to Have a Pure Conscience

The conscience is the leading part of the spirit. We need to have a good conscience. When our conscience condemns us, we are unable to exercise our spirit properly. We must also have a pure conscience (3:9; 2 Tim. 1:3). Our conscience may be good because it is cleansed from anything sinful, dirty, or evil, but it may not be pure because of our self-seeking motive. A pure conscience is a conscience that is within a heart that cares for nothing but God. As we pointed out in the previous message, a brother may be very good; morally there may be nothing wrong with him. From another angle, however, he may not be pure. His conscience is good, but it is not pure because he is not for God alone but also for something else, such as the mission field, a congregation, a position, or his own glory, honor, and respect. There is nothing morally wrong with his work, but he has no purity because of his many motives. Without a pure conscience, a conscience that is absolutely for God, it is difficult to serve God. In order to serve God, we must have a pure conscience. In 2 Timothy 1:3 Paul said, "I thank God, whom I serve from my forefathers in a pure conscience." For Paul to say this meant that he was seeking only God. We need this kind of a pure conscience.

A Pure Heart Being a Mind, Emotion, and Will That Are Singly for the Lord

First Timothy 1:5 also speaks of a pure heart. The heart is a composition of the mind, emotion, will, and conscience (Matt. 9:4; Heb. 4:12; John 16:22, 6; Acts 11:23; Heb. 10:22). This means that our mind, emotion, will, and conscience must be pure. Every part of our being needs to be pure. Many Christians today like to study the Bible according to its doctrinal teachings, but they have many differing opinions and concepts concerning these teachings. This indicates that their mind, emotion, and will are not pure; that is, they do not have a pure heart. Since their heart is not pure, their conscience also is not pure. In order to have a pure conscience, we must have a pure mind, emotion, and will.

A pure heart is a heart that is single and simple for the Lord. This means that our mind considers nothing but the Lord, our emotion loves nothing but Him, and our will chooses only Him. In our mind, emotion, and will we are for nothing but the Lord and seek only Him. This is to have a pure heart and a pure conscience. Is our mind fully and wholly for God? Does our emotion simply and fully love the Lord? Is our will wholly for God? If we check with ourselves, we will admit that we are not pure. In our mind there is much "traffic" in many directions. Likewise, in our emotion we love the Lord, but we also love many other things. Similarly, our will may be for the Lord in the morning, but at noon it will be for something else, and in the evening it may be for yet another thing. This means that we are not pure in our mind, emotion, and will; that is, we do not have a pure heart.

A Pure Conscience Being Vital for the Exercise of Our Spirit

When all our inward parts are pure, our heart is pure and our conscience is also pure. A pure conscience is vital for the exercise of the spirit. If our conscience is not good, if there is condemnation in our conscience, our spirit will be deadened. If we have condemnation, then regardless how much people encourage us to exercise our spirit, we will be unable to do it. However, we may have a good conscience but not a pure one, so once again our spirit is unable to be strong. Within our conscience there may be the testimony that we are not pure and single for the Lord. What we are seeking is not evil, but it is not the Lord Himself. This kind of condemnation is not rough and coarse but deep, fine, and tender, pointing out to us that we are not fully and purely for the Lord. Even this kind of condemnation weakens our spirit. We may tell others that we are right, but we cannot tell this to our conscience. The more we argue that we are right, the more troubling we will have in our conscience. The wise way is not to argue with our conscience.

We need to be pure in all our inward parts—in our conscience, heart, mind, emotion, and will. If we deal with these inward parts, we will have a pure conscience in a pure heart with a pure will, pure emotion, and pure mind. Then we will be able to exercise our spirit. Otherwise, it will be difficult to exercise our spirit. To exercise our spirit requires a preparation. We must have a spirit of power in our will, of love in our emotion, and of soberness and soundness in our mind. These three inward parts must be under the control of the spirit. Then our heart will be pure, and our conscience will be transparent and crystal clear. It will be easy for us to exercise our spirit, and there will be a free way for our spirit to be released.

Chapter Three

EXERCISING OUR SPIRIT TO PRAY AND TO DEAL WITH THE WORD OF GOD

Scripture Reading: 1 Tim. 2:1-3, 8-14; 2 Tim. 2:22; 1 Tim. 1:3-4; 4:6-7; 2 Tim. 4:4; 3:16; 1 Tim. 1:10; 4:6; 6:3; 2 Tim. 1:13; 4:3; Titus 1:9; 2:1

EXERCISING OUR SPIRIT IN EVERY KIND OF PRAYER

The two Epistles to Timothy speak in a particular way concerning praying and dealing with the word of God for the exercise of our spirit. First Timothy 2:1 through 3 say, "I exhort therefore, first of all, that petitions, prayers, intercessions, thanksgivings be made on behalf of all men; on behalf of kings and all who are in high position, that we may lead a quiet and tranquil life in all godliness and gravity. This is good and acceptable in the sight of our Savior God." Verse 1 speaks of all kinds of prayer, including general prayers and special prayers for particular needs. These prayers should be made not only for one class of people but for all men. Verse 2 indicates that this prayer for all men is related to godliness. In order to exercise our spirit, we need to pray in many ways. Ephesians 6:18 says, "By means of all prayer and petition, praying at every time in spirit and watching unto this in all perseverance and petition concerning all the saints." Prayer and petition must be made in the spirit. To pray in all these ways is the true exercise of the spirit and the real priesthood.

EXERCISING OUR SPIRIT TO PRAY REQUIRING THAT WE DENY THE REASONINGS OF THE MIND

First Timothy 2:8 continues, "I desire therefore that men pray in every place, lifting up holy hands, without wrath and reasoning." Sometimes we are unable to lift up our hands in prayer because they are not holy, separated unto God. To have holy hands requires the exercise of our spirit. Wrath is in the emotion, and reasoning is in the mind. To pray without wrath and reasoning requires that we exercise our spirit, not our natural emotion and mind. However, sometimes we exercise our mind and emotion much more than we exercise our spirit. To reason, question, and dispute is the exercise of the mind. If we would deny our natural mind, our reasonings will not trouble us. We will not care for questions; we will care only for praying in every place.

Questionings come from Satan as the serpent (Gen. 3:1). When a serpent rises up to strike, we may say that he takes the shape of a question mark. Satan as the serpent stirs up questions in the mind. The first time the serpent came to contact human beings was when he stirred up the mind of Eve in Genesis 3. He suggested something to Eve, causing her to exercise her mentality. For this reason, the apostle Paul did not allow women to teach with authority in the church. In 1 Timothy 2:8 Paul says simply that men should pray in every place. In the following verses, however, he instructs that the women also should pray, but he adds some further requirements. Verses 11 through 14 continue, "Let a woman learn in quietness in all subjection; but I do not permit a woman to teach or to assert authority over a man, but to be in quietness. For Adam was formed first, then Eve; and Adam was not deceived; but the woman, having been quite deceived, has fallen into transgression." Eve was deceived because she improperly exercised her mind. Because teaching requires the proper exercise of the mind, it is better for sisters simply to pray. The sisters do not have the ground to teach, because it requires the exercise of the mind; rather, they have the ground to pray, which is to exercise the spirit.

Several books of the New Testament contain teachings concerning prayer, but the Epistles to Timothy are unique to show the practice and practical instructions concerning prayer. Second Timothy 2:22 says, "Flee youthful lusts, and pursue righteousness, faith, love, peace with those who call on the Lord out of a pure heart." This verse does not encourage us to pursue with those who merely study the Bible for doctrinal learning. We need to come together not merely for teachings or study but to call on the Lord with a pure heart. To pray by calling on the Lord is the real exercise of the spirit. In order to pray with every kind of prayer, intercession, petition, and thanksgiving on behalf of all men, to pray in every place by raising holy hands, and to pray without wrath in our emotion or reasoning in our mind, we need to exercise our spirit.

DENYING NATURAL SPEAKING TO EXERCISE OUR SPIRIT BY PRAYING

We need the practice of prayer that is according to the instruction in 1 and 2 Timothy. If a brother speaks to us out of the reasonings of his mind, we should not respond with an answer, argument, or suggestion. We should simply say, "Brother, let us pray." We should not exercise our natural mind over what he says. Rather, we need to exercise our spirit to bring his matters in prayer to the Lord. We should know only to contact the Lord by exercising our spirit. Then we should pursue the things that are pleasing to the Lord with all those who call on Him out of a pure heart. In order to exercise our spirit to minister as priests, we need to learn to pray in this way. I long to see the day when all the brothers do not care for discussing, debating, arguing, or even merely studying. Rather, whether in their homes, in the meeting hall, or in any place, they know only to pray. If we all practice this kind of prayer, we will have the real priesthood among us. Then we will see the move of the Lord in a powerful and prevailing way. The Lord is recovering the priesthood of prayer by the exercise of the spirit.

We should not exercise our natural mind to discuss, debate, argue, question, or doubt. Likewise, we should not have a wrathful emotion. We should do only one thing: pray with every kind of prayer, petition, intercession, and thanksgiving not only for one class of people but for all men. We are too indifferent concerning many things. How many times have we prayed for the President, the governor of our state, and the world situation? We need to pray that we may have the opportunity to lead a peaceful life in godliness. However, I am not encouraging you to pray mainly for certain things. I am encouraging you to exercise your spirit. Whenever we come together, we should not talk too much. Sometimes this kind of talk is simply gossip. We should forget about everything else and simply pray. If we find ourselves speaking of people and families, we should immediately say, "Let us not talk anymore. Let us pray for them." If we are concerned for a certain brother or sister, we should pray rather than talk. We must learn to pray. I long to see that one day on this earth there would be the church with many dear ones who do not gossip or merely talk but simply pray.

Today there is too much natural talk among the Lord's children. Someone may ask, "How are things in Taiwan?" or "How is that brother?" or "How is his wife and mother-in-law?" After asking all these questions, he may go to spread the knowledge he has gained to others. No one is able to repeat what he hears exactly. He will either leave out something or add something, and eventually he will spread rumors. Then death will follow. This kind of talk deadens the spirits of the saints and the church. We must all learn the lesson to stop our talking. Our mouth was created by God not for talking in this way but for praying.

Gossip may be compared to myths. Paul uses the word *myths* several times in 1 and 2 Timothy. First Timothy 1:3 and 4 say, "Even as I exhorted you, when I was going into Macedonia, to remain in Ephesus in order that you might charge certain ones not to teach different things nor to give heed to myths and unending genealogies, which produce questionings rather than God's economy, which is in faith." Verses 6 and 7 of chapter 4 say, "If you lay these things before the brothers, you will be a good minister of Christ Jesus, being nourished with the words of the faith and of the good teaching which you have closely followed. But the profane and old-womanish myths refuse, and exercise yourself unto godliness." Second Timothy 4:4 says, "They will turn away their ear from the truth and will be turned aside to myths." We must learn to refuse gossip, myths, and tales. These things only cause us to exercise our fallen, natural mind.

We should receive this word not as a mere teaching but as loving fellowship. I long to see that in the Lord's recovery the church would be a group not of talking people but of praying people. Whenever we meet together, we should leave all our talking and always concentrate on praying. We should say, "Brothers and sisters, let us pray." We should pray at every time in spirit for all men with every kind of prayer, petition, intercession, and giving of thanks, and we should do this with those who call on the Lord out of a pure heart. This is the proper way to exercise our spirit.

RECEIVING THE WORD AS THE BREATH OF GOD

Second Timothy 3:16 is a unique passage among all the books of the New Testament. This verse says, "All Scripture is God-breathed and profitable for teaching, for conviction, for correction, for instruction in righteousness." All the words of the Bible are God's divine breathing. This is a matter of the Spirit in our spirit. Because the Word of God is not merely for teaching, we cannot fully apprehend it by exercising our mind. The mind is not sufficient. We need to exercise our spirit to apprehend the word, because the word is spiritual breath, the very breath of God. When we read the Word, we must learn how to breathe it in, not merely to understand it. It is a wrong concept that when we read the Word we mainly need to understand it. The word of God is spiritual food and drink (Matt. 4:4; 1 Pet. 2:2; Jer. 15:16; Psa. 119:103; Job 23:12; John 6:63). It is not necessary to understand food; we need only to eat it. The Bible is not mainly for our understanding. It is for us to breathe in.

EXERCISING OUR SPIRIT TO RECEIVE THE HEALTHY WORDS AND HEALTHY TEACHING

First Timothy 1:10 speaks of things that are "opposed to the healthy teaching." Something that is healthy is related to life. We can compare healthy teaching to today's "health food." Health food is not something for us to understand in our mind. It is for the health of our physical life. In the same way, the healthy teachings of the Bible are not firstly teachings for the mind but nourishment for the spirit. Verse 6 of chapter 4 says, "If you lay these things before the brothers, you will be a good minister of Christ Jesus, being nourished with the words of the faith and of the good teaching which you have closely followed." We are nourished with the words of the faith, not merely taught by them. There is a difference between being merely taught by the word and being nourished by the word. Many Christians are only taught by the word without being nourished. We must learn to be nourished by the word of God. The word must be healthy teaching to us, not merely "sound doctrine" for the mind. Healthy teachings are for our spiritual health.

Verse 3 of chapter 6 says, "If anyone teaches different things and does not consent to healthy words, those of our Lord Jesus Christ, and the teaching which is according to godliness." The living and healthy words, the words that are good for our spiritual health, are the words of our Lord Jesus Christ and the teaching that is according to godliness. This is a matter of life, not of knowledge. Many in today's Christianity speak of sound doctrine. It is not wrong to speak in this way but neither is it entirely right. We need the word that is healthy for life, not merely sound for our mind.

Second Timothy 1:13 says, "Hold a pattern of the healthy words that you have heard from me, in the faith and love which are in Christ Jesus," and 4:3 says, "For the time will come when they will not tolerate the healthy teaching; but according to their own lusts they will heap up to themselves teachers, having itching ears." Those with itching ears care only to hear; they do not seek the healthy word, the word that nourishes the spiritual life and is good for spiritual health. Titus 1:9 says, "Holding to the faithful word, which is according to the teaching of the apostles, that he may be able both to exhort by the healthy teaching and to convict those who oppose," and 2:1 says, "But you, speak the things which are fitting to the healthy teaching." In the Epistles to Timothy and Titus, which are among the final writings of the apostle Paul, he stresses healthy words and healthy teaching. This is because at his time there were many who were teaching things that may have seemed to be good but were not healthy and did not minister life to others. This warns us to take care of our speaking. The word we speak must be healthy; it must minister life to others and be full of spiritual nourishment. The messages we give may pass on knowledge without nourishment. They may be sound but not healthy. What we need is the healthy word.

In order to have healthy teachings we must learn to exercise our spirit. If we exercise our mind when we listen to a message, we may admire the message as being an eloquent word with interesting illustrations from a good speaker. However, if we exercise our spirit, we may discern that the eloquent speaking and good illustrations are a worldly speaking without any life. Although another brother may have no eloquence and his utterance is awkward, we may sense that in his speaking there is the nourishing, ministering life. This latter speaking is not merely a "sound teaching"; it is a healthy word. If we come to the meetings to seek healthy teachings, we must exercise our spirit, not merely our mind.

We may discern and appreciate a message either in the mind or in the spirit. If we discern a message in our spirit, we will not care whether or not it is eloquent. We will care only that it ministers life and nourishment. Sometimes people appreciate a certain message simply because they are in the mind. They appreciate a good speaker that gives a good, eloquent message. However, there may be no life in that message. It may be "sound" but not healthy. In contrast, though, we have often seen certain brothers ministering in a very awkward way, but in their speaking we could sense life, nourishment, and something healthy.

We should seek the healthy word of the Bible, not merely sound doctrinal teaching. In order to apprehend something healthy from the Bible, we must learn to exercise our spirit. Whenever we read the Bible, we should pray with what we read and understand, receiving God's word by means of all prayer (Eph. 6:17-18). To pray in this way is to exercise our spirit to touch the word of God. If we do this, we will receive not simply something for our mind but the healthy word for the nourishment of our spirit. As we saw in the previous messages, in order to exercise our spirit we first need to deal with all our inward parts—our mind, emotion, will, heart, and conscience. Second, we need to pray with petitions, prayers, intercessions, and thanksgivings to God, praying for all men and in every place without wrath or reasoning and with all those who call on the Lord out of a pure heart. Third, we need to deal with the word of God in order to take it as healthy food. Whether we read a spiritual book, listen to a message, or come to contact the word of God directly, we must learn to exercise our spirit to receive something healthy for our spirit. We must learn to receive a healthy word, a word that is full of nourishment, not merely a sound or correct word. All day long we need the healthy word, just as our physical body needs healthy food.

Many Christians today are receiving only doctrinal teaching, not healthy food from the word. According to the medical doctors, the best way to have a long physical life is to exercise by walking and to eat properly. Every day we need to be nourished by the word as our healthy food and to exercise to "walk" spiritually (1 Tim. 4:6-7). We need to take care of the inward parts of our being, pray, and receive the healthy, nourishing word of God. This is the right way to exercise our spirit. This is dealt with in a clear, definite, and full way in the two Epistles to Timothy.

Chapter Four

EXERCISING OUR SPIRIT TO PRAY BY THE CLEANSING OF THE BLOOD AND THE SENSE OF THE ANOINTING

Scripture Reading: Heb. 9:14; 10:19-22; 1 John 1:7; 2:27; 1 Thes. 5:16-22; 1 Tim. 2:8; Eph. 6:18

APPLYING THE CLEANSING OF THE BLOOD OF CHRIST FOR THE EXERCISE OF OUR SPIRIT

Being Exposed in the Fellowship and Sensing Our Need of the Blood of Christ

For the exercise of our spirit we need the cleansing of the blood of Christ. First John 1:7 says, "If we walk in the light as He is in the light, we have fellowship with one another, and the blood of Jesus His Son cleanses us from every sin." To exercise our spirit is to have fellowship with the Lord and also with the saints in the presence of the Lord. In the Lord's presence we are in the light. God is light (v. 5), the churches are the lampstands (Rev. 1:11-12, 20), and the saints are the light of the world (Matt. 5:14). Because of this, we are often exposed in the church. Darkness veils, but light exposes. When we are away from the church, everything may seem fine because everything is hidden, covered, and veiled under darkness, but when we come back to the church, the church as the lampstand shines and we are spontaneously exposed.

Whenever we contact God, the church, or the saints, we are enlightened. We can test this in our experience. The more we contact worldly persons, the more we may be in darkness. On the contrary, when we go to contact the brothers and sisters, we are enlightened even while we are on the way to see them. Even before we meet the saints, we already have the feeling that we are wrong concerning certain matters. Then as we come into the presence of the saints, we are under more enlightenment even before we begin to speak. When we are in the fellowship either with the Lord directly or with the church or the saints, we are in the light. This light exposes us, and we are not able to hide from it. Therefore, we need the cleansing of the Lord's blood.

The more we exercise our spirit, the more we enter into fellowship, are under the light, and sense how much we need the blood to cleanse us. In 1 John 1:7 the fellowship, the light, and the blood are related to one another. If we are in the fellowship, we are in the light, and under the light we need the blood to cleanse us. If we do not apply the cleansing blood, our conscience will be dirty and under condemnation. Then our evil conscience will bother us and break the fellowship, and we will not be able to exercise our spirit. Therefore, for the exercise of our spirit we need the cleansing of the blood.

Applying the Blood of Christ to Enter into Our Spirit as the Holy of Holies

Hebrews 9:14 says, "How much more will the blood of Christ, who through the eternal Spirit offered Himself without blemish to God, purify our conscience from dead works to serve the living God?" By the blood our conscience is purged not only from evil works but also from dead works. Verse 19 of chapter 10 says, "Having therefore, brothers, boldness for entering the Holy of Holies in the blood of Jesus," and verse 22 continues, "Let us come forward to the Holy of Holies with a true heart in full assurance of faith, having our hearts sprinkled from an evil conscience and having our bodies washed with pure water." The Holy of Holies today is our human spirit. Because we are sinful, in the old nature, and in the flesh, there is no other way to enter into our spirit and remain in the spirit than through the blood of Christ.

If we are careless with God and our fellowship with Him, we may not sense that we are sinful, but if we care for our fellowship with the Lord and desire to enter into the Holy of Holies, we will immediately sense a condemnation within. This is because regardless of how spiritual we may be, we are still in the old nature, the self, the soul, and the flesh. If we mean business with the Lord to come into His presence, we will sense that we need the cleansing blood. Sometimes we may not sense a particular problem, but we may still have a general sense that we are dirty because we are still in the old nature. Therefore, we need the blood to cleanse us. It is through the blood and by the blood that we can enter into the Holy of Holies, that is, into our spirit.

Certain Christian hymns say that the blood cleanses our heart. It is more accurate to say that according to Hebrews 9:14 the blood purifies our conscience. Whenever we have a feeling that we are sinful or wrong, our conscience is dirty and needs the blood to purify it. Christ shed His blood on the cross to meet all the requirements of God's righteousness, holiness, and glory. Then this blood was brought into heaven itself to be sprinkled before the face of God for our forgiveness and redemption (vv. 23-24). Our conscience within us corresponds to God in heaven. When God in heaven condemns, the conscience within us also condemns, and when God in heaven releases, our conscience also releases. Therefore, when the blood was sprinkled in the presence of God, our conscience was also sprinkled and released. For this reason we have a good conscience, and we have peace in our conscience.

If we do not know how to apply the blood, we will not know how to exercise our spirit. Whenever we come to exercise our spirit to contact the Lord, it is vital that we apply the blood to cleanse our conscience. God is righteous, holy, and in glory, but we are sinful, evil, dirty, worldly, common, and short of His glory (Rom. 3:23). Therefore, we need the blood to bridge the gap between us and God so that we may come into His presence by exercising our spirit to contact Him. We must learn how to apply the blood. Through the blood of Christ we have freedom, peace, boldness, and victory. Without the application of the blood, Satan, the enemy, the subtle one, constantly accuses us of being wrong in certain matters and with certain persons. When we apply the blood, it gives us the victory over the accusations of the evil one, and we immediately have the peace within and the boldness to contact the Lord (Rev. 12:11).

EXERCISING OUR SPIRIT BY CARING FOR THE FEELING OF THE ANOINTING

In 1 John 1 there is the cleansing of the blood, and in chapter 2 there is the anointing. First John 2:27 says, "As for you, the anointing which you have received from Him abides in you, and you have no need that anyone teach you; but as His anointing teaches you concerning all things and is true and is not a lie, and even as it has taught you, abide in Him." The anointing is the Holy Spirit as the oil moving and working in us (Exo. 30:25). The living, divine anointing within us is the constant moving, working, inspiring, and enlightening of the indwelling Spirit of Christ. In order to exercise our spirit, we must not only apply the blood of Christ but also take care of this anointing. This means that we must go along with the inner moving and working of the Spirit.

For the sake of the exercise of our spirit, we need to learn the lesson of rejecting our natural mind and caring for the anointing. It is often more difficult to forget something than to remember it. If a brother offends us, for example, we may remember this for a long time. If we exercise our mind in this way, we will neglect the inner anointing. Instead, we need to forsake our natural mind and care only for the moving and working of the anointing Spirit in our spirit. We may further illustrate how to care for the anointing in the following way. In the afternoon we may be burdened when we remember that we need to minister the word in the evening meeting. Therefore, we may go to the Lord with the intention of praying for the meeting and the message. However, when we go to the Lord, deep within our spirit there may be a feeling, consciousness, or sense, through the moving of the Holy Spirit within us, that we should pray for something else. If at this time we continue to pray according to our memory, we will exercise only our mind in our prayer. This is wrong. Rather, we need to drop that burden, forget about the meeting and the message, and go along with the inner anointing to pray according to what we feel deep within. This is a prayer in the exercise of the spirit. We all must learn this lesson.

We must apply the blood and care for the anointing. First John is a book concerning the fellowship of the divine life. It tells us that in order to maintain the fellowship we need the cleansing of the blood on the negative side and the anointing on the positive side. Only these two—the cleansing and the anointing—can maintain us in the proper fellowship, a fellowship not only with the Lord but also with the church and with the saints. We need always to apply the blood and to care for the anointing.

PRAYING UNCEASINGLY BY THE EXERCISE OF OUR SPIRIT

First Thessalonians 5:16-22 says, "Always rejoice, unceasingly pray, in everything give thanks; for this is the will of God in Christ Jesus for you. Do not quench the Spirit; do not despise prophecies, but prove all things. Hold fast to what is good; abstain from every kind of evil." According to the sequence of all the items mentioned in this passage, the focus is on praying unceasingly. If we do not pray without ceasing, it is difficult to rejoice always. In order to be continually joyful, we need to pray unceasingly. To give thanks not only in certain things but in everything also requires that we pray. We need to pray by giving thanks to the Lord in everything and for everything. Likewise, in order not to quench the Spirit we need to pray. Many times the Spirit of prayer and intercession within us inspires us to pray, but we may be lazy and idle. If we do not pray, we will quench the Spirit. By praying we are able to avoid quenching the Spirit. Verse 20 tells us not to despise prophecies. Prophecies here are not predictions. Rather, to prophesy is to speak for God or speak forth God. If we pray without ceasing, we will respect the word spoken for God by any member. Similarly, to prove all things, to hold fast to what is good, and to abstain from every kind of evil also require that we pray. All the matters in these verses are focused on our unceasing prayer.

Verse 17 tells us to pray unceasingly, and 1 Timothy 2:8 tells us to pray in every place. To pray in every place is a matter of space, and to pray unceasingly is a matter of time. Regarding space, we need to pray in every place, and regarding time, we need to pray unceasingly. Ephesians 6:18 says, "By means of all prayer and petition, praying at every time in spirit." These three verses tell us to pray in every place, pray unceasingly, and pray in spirit. If we do not pray in the spirit, we will not be able to pray in every place and unceasingly. If we pray in the spirit and with the spirit, we will be able to pray wherever we are and at any time. While we are talking, eating, and driving, we will still be able to pray because our praying is in the spirit.

Not Waiting but Taking the Initiative to Pray

A certain "spiritual" teaching says that we should not take the initiative to pray, but rather that we must wait on the Lord until He inspires us to pray. It is right to say that we should never pray by ourselves; we must pray by the Lord in our spirit. However, it is not right to say that we must wait until the Lord initiates a prayer. Rather, we should pray unceasingly. There is no need to wait. The Lord has already taken the initiative, and now He is waiting for us to cooperate and coordinate with Him. Wherever we are and at any time, we should not wait. We must take the initiative to open ourselves to the Lord and coordinate with Him to pray.

When we come to the meetings, we should not wait to pray. Instead, we should be prepared to pray. None of the members of a basketball team wait to play after they are on the court. All the members take the initiative and begin to play. This is the way we should be in the meetings. To wait is to be overly spiritual. Do not wait. We should immediately open our spirit and mouth to utter something from within. The way to exercise our spirit is to learn not to wait but to open ourselves and pray unceasingly. We may take the initiative because the Lord is already waiting for us. The Psalms often tell us to wait on the Lord (Psa. 25:5; 27:14; 40:1; 130:5-6). However, to wait on the Lord and to wait to pray are two different matters. There is no verse that tells us to wait to pray. We should pray in every place and at every time.

We may compare praying to driving a car. We do not drive a car by taking the steering wheel and waiting for the car to start. Rather, everything in the car is ready, so we simply need to start it. Our prayer is in the same principle. Everything is ready for us to begin to pray, so there is no excuse not to pray. This requires much practice, but because we do not adequately practice to pray in this way, it is difficult for us to open our mouths when we come into a meeting. The way to practice the priesthood is simply to pray at every time by exercising our spirit. We must always exercise our spirit and be ready to pray.

Learning to Open to Others for the Sake of Our Prayer

For the sake of our prayer, we must learn to always be open to others. It is easy to open to the Lord when we pray by ourselves, but it is not as easy to open ourselves to others. We may even pray with a small group, but we may not be able to pray in a meeting. To open ourselves to the Lord and to others requires exercise and practice. This is vital. In order to exercise our spirit we need to practice until our spirit is strong enough that we have no fear before anyone or in any situation. A brother in Shanghai once told me, "When I was in a small church in a village of my own countrymen, I was able to pray freely. However, when I came to Shanghai where there are many spiritual brothers, I was no longer able to pray." Some of us today who once were in a smaller locality also may find it difficult to pray where there are many elderly and spiritual brothers. This is wrong. We need to practice and exercise so that regardless of the place, time, situation, or persons present we can always open ourselves to pray. If we do not do this, we will be very limited in the exercise of our spirit.

Our prayer meetings are sometimes not balanced. Some of the brothers find it easy to open themselves to pray, but many are not open. This can be compared to a basketball team in which only two members pass the ball to each other while the other three are inactive. The right way is that all the members play as a team. When we come together with one hundred people to pray, everyone must open his mouth. We all come to pray, not to sit silently. There is no excuse for not praying. However, some may be afraid to pray unless they have the assurance that there will be many loud "amens" to their prayer. This is because of pride. We need to forget our pride. If we would all learn how to exercise our spirit, everyone would pray in the prayer meetings.

In certain places where we conducted a formal training, some of the saints were helped by signing an agreement that they would pray in the prayer meetings. To be regulated in this way was effective to help them to open themselves to pray. Instead of encouraging you to sign an agreement, however, I would beg you to realize that the church needs the priesthood, and the priestly service is mainly to burn the incense by praying (Luke 1:8-10). The priesthood is a praying ministry, and to pray requires the exercise of the spirit. Without the exercise of our spirit in prayer, we cannot practically be in the priesthood. Rather, we will not be able to function for the building up of the church.

A meeting in which there are no speakers yet everyone prays is more edifying and satisfying than a meeting in which a few speak and everyone else is silent. This is because a meeting in which everyone prays requires all the members to exercise their spirit. When we all exercise our spirit, the Holy Spirit has a free way to flow. Satan, the subtle one, knows that if we all exercise and release our spirit, he will be defeated. Because of this he strategically tries to choke the spirits of the saints. If Satan can choke our spirit, we are all finished and he has succeeded. Therefore, we need to fight the battle. Whenever we come to a meeting we must learn to exercise and release our spirit and always be ready to pray.

We must look to the Lord that we will be helped, adjusted, and balanced. We must learn to apply the blood, go along with the inner anointing, and be bold to open ourselves and take the initiative to pray, regardless of the place, time, and persons present. There is no need to take care of a particular situation or have an object for our prayer. We simply should open our spirit to say something to the Lord according to the inner sense. Whatever we sense deep within is what we should utter.

A Testimony of Prayer

As Christians we may prefer to come together to listen to a good speaker, talk, or study the Bible. If we announce that a great speaker will come to our meeting, the meeting place will be crowded, but if we say that the following meeting will be a time of prayer, only a few may come. We must fight against this trend. When we come together, we should not talk much. Rather, we should exercise our spirit to pray, each one in turn. If we practice this, we will see a positive result. This is the exercise we need today.

When our work first began in Los Angeles in December of 1962, I came together with two other brothers five or six days a week for three weeks to pray from 8:30 A.M. until noon. We did not talk much, and we did not have a particular object for our prayer. We simply knelt and prayed, each one in turn. After those three weeks of prayer, we had our first winter conference. Already in that conference we began to see the Lord's answers to our prayers. I can testify that in the years since that time, we have seen many answers to those prayers. We must all learn to practice the exercise of our spirit by opening ourselves to pray in any situation and in any kind of meeting. Our spirit must be strong, living, and ready to open with others to pray.

Chapter Five

OUR REGENERATED SPIRIT AS OUR PERSON WITH OUR SOUL AS ITS ORGAN

Scripture Reading: Rom. 7:8, 11, 17, 20, 23; Matt. 16:21-26; Eph. 2:1, 5; Col. 2:13; 1 Cor. 2:14-15; 2 Cor. 4:16; Eph. 3:16; 4:22-24; Col. 3:9-10; Rom. 6:6; Gal. 5:24; Heb. 2:14

In the Bible, the word *soul* may be understood in several ways. First, man himself is a soul. Genesis 2:7 says, "Jehovah God formed man from the dust of the ground and breathed into his nostrils the breath of life, and man became a living soul." God formed a body for man from the dust of the ground, but the breath of life that God breathed into man's body became the spirit of man, the human spirit (Job 32:8; Prov. 20:27). As a result, man became a living soul. First Corinthians 15:45a says, "So also it is written, 'The first man, Adam, became a living soul,'" and referring to the seventy persons in the house of Jacob, Deuteronomy 10:22 says, "Your fathers went down into Egypt as seventy souls" (cf. Gen. 46:27; Exo. 1:5). All these verses tell us that man himself is a soul. In addition, *soul* in the Bible refers to the soulish part of the human being and also to the soulish functions of man.

Soul also refers to the soulish life of man, because the soulish part of man is the place where his human life is. In the New Testament, the Greek word for *soul* is *psuche,* which is also translated as *soul-life,* as in Matthew 16:25-26, which says, "Whoever wants to save his soul-life shall lose it; but whoever loses his soul-life for My sake shall find it. For what shall a man be profited if he gains the whole world, but forfeits his soul-life? Or what shall a man give in exchange for his soul-life?" Similarly, John 12:25 says, "He who loves his soul-life loses it; and he who hates his soul-life in this world shall keep it unto eternal life." Thus, in various verses of the Bible *soul* denotes man himself, the soulish part of man, the soulish functions, and the soulish life.

THE PERSON OF FALLEN MAN BEING HIS SOUL

The person of fallen man is his soul, having an outward and inward organ. The physical body, which was made from the dust of the ground, is the outward organ to contact the physical, material world. The spirit, which came from the spiritual breath of life, is the inward organ to contact the Lord in the spiritual realm. We should not consider that the person of the natural man is either his body or his spirit. Both of these are simply organs; the soul is the person. Because the soul is the being, the person, of man, within the soul is man's self, his personality. Likewise, within every being there is a life. The life of the natural man is neither in his body nor his spirit. The human life is in the soul.

THE BODY BEING RUINED BY THE FALL TO BECOME THE FLESH

At the time of the fall, Satan as sin came into man's body through man's eating of the fruit of the tree of the knowledge of good and evil (Gen. 3:1-6). Romans 7:17 says, "Now then it is no longer I that work it out but sin that dwells in me." According to this verse and verses 8, 11, and 20, sin dwells in us and operates in us, and according to 6:12 and 14, sin reigns in our mortal body and lords it over us. These verses indicate that sin is a person, the embodiment of Satan with his evil nature. In the New Testament Satan is called "the evil one" (Matt. 13:19, 38; John 17:15; 1 John 2:13-14; 5:18-19). In Greek this phrase is literally "the evil." Sin and the evil are Satan himself.

Romans 7:23 tells us where this sin dwells: "I see a different law in my members, warring against the law of my mind and making me a captive to the law of sin which is in my members." Sin dwells in the members of our body. This means that Satan entered into fallen man through his body. Every kind of lust is in the body because the source of lust—Satan, the evil one—is in the body, that is, in the flesh. Originally, the body was something good and pure, but since Satan came into it and damaged it, the body was changed in nature to become the flesh. Genesis 6:3 says, "And Jehovah said, My Spirit will not strive with man forever, for he indeed is flesh." The body is the flesh because it was corrupted and ruined when Satan entered into it.

THE SOUL BEING DAMAGED UNDER THE INFLUENCE OF THE FLESH TO BECOME THE SELF

Moreover, when man—the being, the soul—came under the influence and control of the flesh, the soul too was damaged. Just as the body became the flesh, the soul became the self. Because the soul came under the control of the flesh and was influenced by the flesh, the person of the soul became self-centered, the self. Because Satan took our body as his base in order to invade our soul, sin is in our body, the ruined body became the flesh, and the soul was damaged, influenced, and led into captivity to become the self. All these terms—*Satan, sin, flesh,* and *self*—are very negative.

Matthew 16:21 through 26 illustrates the ground that Satan has in the human soul. These verses say, "From that time Jesus began to show to His disciples that He must go to Jerusalem and suffer many things from the elders and chief priests and scribes and be killed and on the third day be raised. And Peter took Him aside and began to rebuke Him, saying, God be merciful to You, Lord! This shall by no means happen to You! But He turned and said to Peter, Get behind Me, Satan! You are a stumbling block to Me, for you are not setting your mind on the things of God, but on the things of men. Then Jesus said to His disciples, If anyone wants to come after Me, let him deny himself and take up his cross and follow Me. For whoever wants to save his soul-life shall lose it; but whoever loses his soul-life for My sake shall find it. For what shall a man be profited if he gains the whole world, but forfeits his soul-life? Or what shall a man give in exchange for his soul-life?"

In verse 23 the Lord rebuked Satan, but in verse 24 He did not tell the disciples to deny Satan; He told them to deny the self. Then in verses 25 and 26 He went on to speak of the soul-life. Satan, the self, and the soul-life are used here interchangeably. Satan is mingled with the self, and the satanic self is the embodiment of the soul-life. In other words, the soul has a life, and the embodiment of the soulish life is the satanic self. Therefore, we may say that the soulish life is mingled with Satan.

THE SPIRIT BEING DEADENED BECAUSE OF THE FALL BUT PRESERVED FROM SATAN'S INVASION

What then happened to the spirit? On one hand, the spirit was deadened because of the fall. Ephesians 2:1 and 5 and Colossians 2:13 tell us that we were dead in offenses and sins. This does not mean that man is dead in his body or in his soul. Rather, man is very active in the body and soul, but the worldly people, the unbelievers, are deadened and dormant in their spirit. They have a human spirit, but it is deadened and out of function. On the other hand, God has preserved man's human spirit so that Satan could never come into it. Although Satan took the physical body as his base to invade the soul, he was not able to enter into the spirit and take it over. Ephesians 2 tells us that Satan, the evil one, operated in the sons of disobedience, but it does not indicate that he invaded their spirit. As we have shown, Satan took the body as his base, invaded the soul, and even mingled himself with the soul, but he has no ground in the human spirit. It is as if God drew a boundary around the human spirit and told Satan, "For the time being, you have gained man's body as your base, and you have even invaded his soul and mingled yourself with it. However, you must stop here."

OUR REGENERATED SPIRIT INDWELT BY CHRIST BECOMING OUR NEW PERSON

Man with the soul as his person has a body as an outward organ and a spirit as an inward organ. The body was taken over and ruined by Satan as sin to become the flesh, the soul was mingled with Satan to become the self, and the spirit was deadened. Satan, sin, flesh, self, and death all became the real situation and condition of fallen man. However, when we believed in the Lord Jesus as our Savior and in His death for us, we were forgiven, justified, and reconciled to God. All the problems between us and God were solved. At this point, the Lord Jesus as life came into our deadened spirit. Our spirit was made alive, and death was swallowed up. Now in our spirit we have another life, not the *psuche,* the soulish life, but the *zoe,* the divine life (Rom. 8:10). In this way we were not only enlivened but born again. We became a new person, a new being, not in the soul but in the spirit (John 3:6).

However, there is now a problem. Before we were born again, we were only one man in the soul, but now we have two men, one in the soul and the other in the spirit. The first is the soulish man, the old man, the outer man, and the other is the spiritual man, the new man, the inner man. First Corinthians 2:14 and 15 say, "A soulish man does not receive the things of the Spirit of God, for they are foolishness to him and he is not able to know them because they are discerned spiritually. But the spiritual man discerns all things, but he himself is discerned by no one." In these two verses we have the soulish man and the spiritual man. We must be clear that the soulish man cannot know or receive the things of God, but the spiritual man discerns them. Second Corinthians 4:16 says, "Therefore we do not lose heart; but though our outer man is decaying, yet our inner man is being renewed day by day." In this verse there is the outer man and the inner man. The outer man is the man in the soul, and the inner man is the man in the spirit. Ephesians 3:16 also speaks of the inner man, saying, "That He would grant you, according to the riches of His glory, to be strengthened with power through His Spirit into the inner man."

Satan, the Flesh, the Soul-life, the Self, and the Old Man All Having Been Crucified

Formerly we were the soulish man, and we could live only by the life of this man because we did not have another life. However, Christ has come into us to be our life, regenerated us, and brought us forth as the new man. Since we have another person and another life, we must live by this spiritual man, this new man, this inner man, and no longer by the old man, the soulish man. Romans 6:6 says, "Knowing this, that our old man has been crucified with Him in order that the body of sin might be annulled, that we should no longer serve sin as slaves." Similarly, Galatians 5:24 tells us that the flesh also has been crucified. Moreover, Hebrews 2:14 says, "Since therefore the children have shared in blood and flesh, He also Himself in like manner partook of the same, that through death He might destroy him who has the might of death, that is, the devil." Therefore, our old man, the soul-life, the self, and Satan have all been crucified. Now our only problem is that although the Lord has "crossed out" all these negative items, we may still treasure them and live by the old man. We need to live by the new man, the spiritual man, which is our regenerated spirit indwelt by Christ. This is the reason that our soul as the outer man is being consumed and our spirit as the inner man is being renewed day by day.

The Function of the Soul Being Renewed to Be Used by Our Spirit

The soulish life is different from the function of the soul. Originally our soul was our person, and our spirit was the organ. Now there has been a great change—our spirit has become our person, and our soul is the organ. The soulish life, nature, and self have been crucified but not the function of the soul. The function of the soul in thinking, loving, and deciding remains with us in order to be renewed. This is the reason that Romans 12:2 tells us to be transformed by the renewing of the mind. When the mind is renewed, the emotion and will also follow to be renewed.

An organ does not have the right or ground to live or make a decision, but a person has every right and ground. Today we must live not by the soul but by the spirit as our person, using the soul as the organ. Our soul must simply be the organ for our spirit as the person. We should not give our soul the ground and right within us. If our soul decides to go somewhere, we should tell it, "Do not propose anything to me; you have no right. You are merely an organ to me. When I want to go somewhere, I will tell you, and you must come with me to be my organ." Our spirit as our person has the right and ground to propose something but not our soul. We should not treat our soul as our life, person, or being. Rather, we must realize that the soul is simply an organ for our spirit as our person.

Living by Our Spirit as Our Person

Our soul has no more right or ground because it is no longer our life, being, and person. It is simply an organ. Therefore, we must live not by the soul but by the spirit. We should love things not according to the soul but according to the spirit. Formerly the soul was our person, but today our person is our regenerated spirit indwelt by Christ. Sometimes our soul may demand that we hate a certain person, but we should tell it, "Be silent! You have no right to say this. When I need to use you as my organ to hate something, I will tell you. You are only the organ. My being, person, and life today is my regenerated spirit indwelt by Christ." When we live in the soul, we are living in the self and are involved with Satan, sin, and the flesh, but when we deny the soul, telling it that it has no more right or ground within us, we are delivered from Satan, sin, the flesh, and the self. When we learn to live, walk, and do things in the spirit, we are delivered from many negative matters.

Chapter Six

LIVING, WALKING, AND DOING ALL THINGS IN THE SPIRIT

Scripture Reading: Rom. 8:4; Eph. 6:18; Rev. 1:10; 4:2; 17:3; 21:10; Eph. 1:17; Gal. 6:1; Phil. 2:1; 1 Pet. 3:4

Romans 8:4 says, "That the righteous requirement of the law might be fulfilled in us, who do not walk according to the flesh but according to the spirit." Different translations of the Bible render *spirit* in Romans 8 either with an upper case *S* to designate the Holy Spirit or in lower case to designate our human spirit. According to the usage in the New Testament, the word *spirit* in verse 4 denotes our regenerated human spirit indwelt by and mingled with the Spirit. Christ as the life-giving Spirit is mingled with our regenerated human spirit, and these two spirits are mingled as one (1 Cor. 15:45b; 6:17; Rom. 8:16). We need to walk according to this spirit. Ephesians 6:18 says, "By means of all prayer and petition, praying at every time in spirit." This again is the mingled spirit, our regenerated spirit indwelt by the Spirit of God.

In Revelation 1 John saw the vision of the seven golden lampstands with the Son of Man standing in their midst. Verse 10 says, "I was in spirit on the Lord's Day." Again this refers to the mingled spirit. Prior to the second vision concerning the judgment of the world throughout the ages, 4:2 says, "Immediately I was in spirit." Then at the beginning of the third vision concerning Babylon the Great in chapter 17, verse 3 says, "And he carried me away in spirit," and before the vision of the new heaven and the new earth with the New Jerusalem in chapter 21, verse 10 says, "And he carried me away in spirit." In receiving each of the four major visions of the book of Revelation, John was in spirit.

Ephesians 1:17 says, "That the God of our Lord Jesus

Christ, the Father of glory, may give to you a spirit of wisdom and revelation in the full knowledge of Him." A spirit of wisdom and revelation is the mingled spirit. Galatians 6:1 says, "Brothers, even if a man is overtaken in some offense, you who are spiritual restore such a one in a spirit of meekness, looking to yourself lest you also be tempted." One who is spiritual is one who lives and walks by the Spirit of God, who indwells and is mingled with his regenerated spirit. If we go to restore a fallen brother, we must do it in spirit. Philippians 2:1 says, "If there is therefore any encouragement in Christ, if any consolation of love, if any fellowship of spirit, if any tenderheartedness and compassions." Our fellowship is in the mingled spirit. Lastly, 1 Peter 3:4 says, "But the hidden man of the heart in the incorruptible adornment of a meek and quiet spirit, which is very costly in the sight of God." The hidden man of the heart is our human spirit because the heart, composed of all the parts of the soul plus the conscience, surrounds the spirit. Peter tells us that sisters should adorn themselves with the hidden man, the inner man, the spirit.

LIVING BY DOING ALL THINGS IN THE SPIRIT

All the preceding verses show that we, the regenerated ones, need to walk, live, do things, and have everything in the spirit. We may have the wrong impression that to exercise our spirit is only to pray. To pray is one of the many ways to exercise our spirit, but it is not the only way. We may exercise our spirit in everything we do. When we speak with people, we need to speak by exercising our spirit. When we are angry with someone, we must be angry by exercising our spirit. Of course, if we exercise our spirit, we may not become angry, but if we are angry, we must be able to say that we are angry in the spirit. Then our anger will be justified. Even our love, if it is not in the spirit, is not justified. What matters is not whether we love or hate. What matters is whether we live by the old man or by the new person in our spirit.

Luke 14:25 and 26 say, "There were great crowds going along with Him, and He turned and said to them, If anyone comes to Me and does not hate his own father and mother and wife and children and brothers and sisters, and moreover, even his own soul-life, he cannot be My disciple." What matters today is not loving or hating but whether we do things in the soul or in the spirit, whether we live by the old man or by the new man. To love by the soul is wrong, but to hate by the spirit is right. Once the Lord Jesus became angry in the temple, driving out the moneychangers with a whip and overturning their tables (John 2:14-15). On other occasions He called the Pharisees offspring, or brood, of vipers (Matt. 3:7; 12:34; 23:33). In 1 Corinthians 4:21 the apostle Paul says, "What do you want? Should I come to you with a rod or in love and a spirit of meekness?" Sometimes in our soul, not in our spirit, we are meeker and more gentle than the Lord Jesus and the apostle.

To exercise the spirit is not only to pray. It is to do everything in the spirit. If we have no confirmation or feeling in our spirit when we do or say something, we should not do or say it. The proper way for Christians to live is to consider not whether something is good or bad but whether we are doing it by our self, in the soul, or by the Lord as the life-giving Spirit mingled with our spirit in a subjective way. We must always exercise our spirit. Even when we deal with our family, we must learn to exercise our spirit. Sometimes the spirit restricts us from speaking something to our wife. In such a case we should remain silent. However, when our spirit releases us to say something, we should follow our spirit.

LIVING NOT ACCORDING TO THE TEACHINGS OF RELIGION BUT BY THE SPIRIT

To live by considering what is right and what is wrong is the teaching of religion. Where I was raised in China, many considered that there was no need to receive Christ, since they were already taught right and wrong by Confucius. However, God's salvation is absolutely different from religion. It is not a matter of right or wrong, good or evil. It is a matter of living and doing things by the self in the soul or by Christ in the spirit. To live by the spirit is the mark of God's salvation; this has been missed by religion, but today the Lord is recovering this.

To exercise our spirit by coming together to pray is only a

small part of our daily walk. We need to constantly exercise our spirit. Whatever we do or speak, whoever we contact, and wherever we go, we must do it in the spirit. I have been learning this lesson for more than thirty-five years, yet even today I still fail. We were all born in the soul, raised in the soul, and educated in the soul, and we have practiced to live in the soul continually. Because of this, it is very easy for us to live in the soul. Within our sixteen waking hours, how much do we live, abide, and remain in the spirit? The Lord told us to watch and pray (Matt. 26:41). We need to be watchful that we would not live in the soul and prayerful that we would live in the spirit. If we are not watchful, we will immediately fall back into the soul.

Christianity today has missed the mark, always giving teachings to people. We do not need mere doctrinal teachings. It is sufficient simply to check whether or not we are in spirit. There is no need for us to teach someone to outwardly love his wife. We may simply ask, "Brother, are you in the spirit?" When a brother is in the spirit, he will be right toward his wife. However, if we are not in the spirit, our contact with others is mere soulish or fleshly conversation, not spiritual fellowship. I often realize that even in doing good things I have been too much in the soul and not faithful to remain absolutely in the spirit. For this reason, when I go to the Lord I spend more time to confess than to pray. To remain in the spirit is a real lesson for us. Recently, I have considered before the Lord what the content of my messages should be. I do not care to pass on merely doctrinal knowledge. The more I have been with the Lord, the more I have had the deep feeling that our urgent need is to be brought into the full realization that we must live in the spirit.

DENYING THE NATURAL SOUL TO LIVE IN THE SPIRIT

In all four Gospels the Lord Jesus told us that we need to deny the self and lose our soul-life (Matt. 16:24-25; Mark 8:34-35; Luke 9:23-24; John 12:25). The Epistles also frequently tell us that we need to live, walk, do things, and pray continually in the spirit. In order to see the things of God, have wisdom, and receive revelation, we need to be in the spirit (1 Cor. 2:11-12; Eph. 1:17).

Satan uses two means to improperly develop the human soul. The first way is supernatural, as in Buddhism and Hinduism. These devilish "isms" teach people to exercise their soul in a supernatural way, developing it to contact the evil spirits in the supernatural world. The other way is through contact with the natural world by means of modern education, science, and culture. Education, television, and newspapers are often used by the devil to improperly develop the soul. Because of this, it is difficult for people to turn from the soul to the spirit and to live in the spirit. Some young brothers have come to us to argue whether or not we should play sports. What matters is not sports themselves. What matters is whether we are in the soul or in the spirit. Are we certain that we are in the spirit when we are playing sports? If we can exercise our spirit by praying while we do something, it is fine to do it. However, often while the brothers are playing sports, they realize that they are in the soul. It is not a matter of what we are doing; it is a matter of in what person we do it, in the soul or in the spirit. The issue today is not what we do but simply whether we live by the spirit or by the soul in whatever we do.

EXERCISING THE SPIRIT BEING NOT ONLY TO PRAY BUT TO LIVE, WALK, SPEAK, AND DO EVERYTHING IN THE SPIRIT

To exercise the spirit is not only to pray. If we cannot exercise our spirit in other matters, we will not be able to exercise our spirit in prayer. The reason we sometimes cannot pray and do not have the appetite to pray is that we are soulish, even fleshly. We have left our spirit behind and have not used it for a long time. Medical experts tell us that if we covered our eyes for a number of months, we would lose our function of sight. In the same way, many brothers and sisters set their spirit aside and always use their mind, emotion, will, or simply their physical body. Because they have no exercise of their spirit, their spirit is out of function.

In 1943 I was very sick and was confined to bed for six

months. After these six months I could not get out of bed and stand on my feet. The function of my legs was weakened, and it took me a long time to recover my walking function. Similarly, we may have put aside the function of our spirit. We may talk, argue, reason, debate, discuss, and even quote the Scriptures merely by exercising the soul. Because of this, a church may be poor, weak, and in confusion. This is due simply to one thing: we have neglected our spirit. We should not argue, reason, or talk in the soul but simply exercise our spirit. If we want to argue, we must first exercise our spirit to contact the Lord and consider our argument before Him. We need to come back to the spirit.

To exercise the spirit is not only to pray but to live, walk, speak, and do everything in the spirit. It is to take care of our inner man and always go along with the inner man in all things. If we practice this, it will be easy to pray at any time and in any place, because our spirit will be strong, living, and active. Not only in prayer or in reading the Word but in all matters in our daily life and walk, private or public, we need to always exercise our spirit. If before we come to read the Bible we first prepare ourselves to exercise our spirit, we will see a difference in our reading. Likewise, in all things we should first exercise our spirit. If we want to talk with our wife or with a brother, we must be ready to exercise our spirit. Even to go shopping we need to prepare ourselves by exercising the spirit. If we do this, we will be saved from much of our shopping. We will do many things in a brief and simple way. We do not trust in mere doctrinal teachings, which do not work. Rather, we trust in the practice of exercising the spirit. In whatever we do, we need to exercise our spirit. The one thing that the New Testament charges us to do at every time is to live, walk, pray, receive wisdom and revelation, and do all things in the spirit.

RECEIVING WISDOM AND REVELATION IN SPIRIT

Ephesians 1:17 speaks of a spirit of wisdom and revelation. We cannot receive revelation by arguing with people. The more we argue, debate, or merely study, the more we are blinded.

We should not trust even in our studying. The more we study in our natural mind, the more we are darkened. If we would silence our natural mind and enter into the spirit, we will receive light and revelation in spirit. A brother may not be clear concerning a certain matter, but if he would enter into the spirit, light and revelation will come. Arguments and reasonings get us nowhere, but to enter into the spirit brings in the light.

A husband may feel that he is right and his wife is wrong, and the more he argues, the more he feels he is right. However, if he would stop his arguing and reasoning and enter into the spirit, he will realize that he is wrong, and he will repent, even with tears. Darkness and blindness are in the mind, but light and revelation are in the spirit. Certain Christians say that they are not clear about the practice of the church life. The more they argue, the more they remain in darkness, but if they would enter into the spirit, they will receive light. This is true of all matters.

Sometimes people are bothered by me because when they come to argue about something, I prefer not to join the argument. Whenever I did argue, I regretted it afterward. It is better not to speak in this kind of arguing way. Rather, if we would enter into the spirit and remain in the spirit for a certain time, everything will be clear. We will be clear with our wife, children, parents, the brothers, the sisters, the church, and the work. To be in the mind is not to be clear, but to be in the spirit makes everything crystal clear. John said, "I was in spirit on the Lord's Day....and when I turned, I saw" (Rev. 1:10, 12). As John was in spirit, he saw the entire situation of the church, the world, all the ages, and even eternity. When we simply enter into the spirit, everything is clear. Please try this. If any part of the Word is not clear to you, do not merely try to understand it. Instead, bring what you have read into the spirit, and there you will see the light. Wisdom and revelation are in the spirit. In order to have wisdom we must remain in the spirit. When we are outside of the spirit, we may do many things foolishly, but if we are in the spirit, we will do things with wisdom. All things are clear when we are in spirit.

PRAYING IN THE MEETINGS AND GIVING OTHERS THE OPPORTUNITY TO PRAY

On the one hand, when we come together to pray, we should not wait. The Lord is ready, so we should simply take the initiative to pray. On the other hand, we should give others the opportunity to pray in the meetings. Again, we may use the illustration of a basketball team. It is never right for one player to play while the others are idle. To pray and to give others the opportunity to pray are two sides. Those who pray much should give the opportunity to others, and those who do not pray must learn not to wait. Those who do not "play" should not complain that others play too much. If you wait, the "ball" will go to another player. In the meetings we all must learn to coordinate. This is a help for us to exercise our spirit to pray in the meetings.

About the Author

Witness Lee was born in 1905 in northern China and raised in a Christian family. At age 19 he was fully captured for Christ and immediately consecrated himself to preach the gospel for the rest of his life. Early in his service, he met Watchman Nee, a renowned preacher, teacher, and writer. Witness Lee labored together with Watchman Nee under his direction. In 1934 Watchman Nee entrusted Witness Lee with the responsibility for his publication operation, called the Shanghai Gospel Bookroom.

Prior to the Communist takeover in 1949, Witness Lee was sent by Watchman Nee and his other co-workers to Taiwan to ensure that the things delivered to them by the Lord would not be lost. Watchman Nee instructed Witness Lee to continue the former's publishing operation abroad as the Taiwan Gospel Bookroom, which has been publicly recognized as the publisher of Watchman Nee's works outside China. Witness Lee's work in Taiwan manifested the Lord's abundant blessing. From a mere 350 believers, newly fled from the mainland, the churches in Taiwan grew to 20,000 in five years.

In 1962 Witness Lee felt led of the Lord to come to the United States, settling in California. During his 35 years of service in the U.S., he ministered in weekly meetings and weekend conferences, delivering several thousand spoken messages. Much of his speaking has since been published as over 400 titles. Many of these have been translated into over fourteen languages. He gave his last public conference in February 1997 at the age of 91.

He leaves behind a prolific presentation of the truth in the Bible. His major work, *Life-study of the Bible,* comprises over 25,000 pages of commentary on every book of the Bible from the perspective of the believers' enjoyment and experience of God's divine life in Christ through the Holy Spirit. Witness Lee was the chief editor of a new translation of the New Testament into Chinese called the Recovery Version and directed the translation of the same into English. The Recovery Version also appears in a number of other languages. He provided an extensive body of footnotes, outlines, and spiritual cross references. A radio broadcast of his messages can be heard on Christian radio stations in the United States. In 1965 Witness Lee founded Living Stream Ministry, a non-profit corporation, located in Anaheim, California, which officially presents his and Watchman Nee's ministry.

Witness Lee's ministry emphasizes the experience of Christ as life and the practical oneness of the believers as the Body of Christ. Stressing the importance of attending to both these matters, he led the churches under his care to grow in Christian life and function. He was unbending in his conviction that God's goal is not narrow sectarianism but the Body of Christ. In time, believers began to meet simply as the church in their localities in response to this conviction. In recent years a number of new churches have been raised up in Russia and in many eastern European countries.

OTHER BOOKS PUBLISHED BY

Living Stream Ministry

Titles by Witness Lee:

Abraham—Called by God	0-7363-0359-6
The Experience of Life	0-87083-417-7
The Knowledge of Life	0-87083-419-3
The Tree of Life	0-87083-300-6
The Economy of God	0-87083-415-0
The Divine Economy	0-87083-268-9
God's New Testament Economy	0-87083-199-2
The World Situation and God's Move	0-87083-092-9
Christ vs. Religion	0-87083-010-4
The All-inclusive Christ	0-87083-020-1
Gospel Outlines	0-87083-039-2
Character	0-87083-322-7
The Secret of Experiencing Christ	0-87083-227-1
The Life and Way for the Practice of the Church Life	0-87083-785-0
The Basic Revelation in the Holy Scriptures	0-87083-105-4
The Crucial Revelation of Life in the Scriptures	0-87083-372-3
The Spirit with Our Spirit	0-87083-798-2
Christ as the Reality	0-87083-047-3
The Central Line of the Divine Revelation	0-87083-960-8
The Full Knowledge of the Word of God	0-87083-289-1
Watchman Nee—A Seer of the Divine Revelation ...	0-87083-625-0

Titles by Watchman Nee:

How to Study the Bible	0-7363-0407-X
God's Overcomers	0-7363-0433-9
The New Covenant	0-7363-0088-0
The Spiritual Man 3 volumes	0-7363-0269-7
Authority and Submission	0-7363-0185-2
The Overcoming Life	1-57593-817-0
The Glorious Church	0-87083-745-1
The Prayer Ministry of the Church	0-87083-860-1
The Breaking of the Outer Man and the Release ...	1-57593-955-X
The Mystery of Christ	1-57593-954-1
The God of Abraham, Isaac, and Jacob	0-87083-932-2
The Song of Songs	0-87083-872-5
The Gospel of God 2 volumes	1-57593-953-3
The Normal Christian Church Life	0-87083-027-9
The Character of the Lord's Worker	1-57593-322-5
The Normal Christian Faith	0-87083-748-6
Watchman Nee's Testimony	0-87083-051-1

Available at

Christian bookstores, or contact Living Stream Ministry
2431 W. La Palma Ave. • Anaheim, CA 92801
1-800-549-5164 • www.livingstream.com